The First Family
The Obamas in the White House

Amelie von Zumbusch

PowerKiDS press.

New York

Published in 2010 by The Rosen Publishing Group, Inc.
29 East 21st Street, New York, NY 10010

First Edition

Editors: Nicole Pristash and Maggie Murphy
Book Design: Kate Laczynski
Photo Researcher: Jessica Gerweck

Photo Credits: Cover, p. 1 Joe Raedle/Getty Images; pp. 4, 12 Saul Loeb/AFP/Getty Images; p. 6 Spencer Platt/Getty Images; p. 8 Scott J. Ferrell/Congressional Quarterly/Getty Images; p. 10 Peter Gridley/Getty Images; p. 14 Chip Somodevilla/Getty Images; pp. 16, 18 Mandel Ngan/AFP/Getty Images; p. 20 Charles Ommanney/Getty Images.

Library of Congress Cataloging-in-Publication Data

Zumbusch, Amelie von.
  First family : the Obamas in the White House / Amelie von Zumbusch.
      p. cm. — (Making history: the Obamas)
  Includes index.
 ISBN 978-1-4358-9389-4 (library binding) — ISBN 978-1-4358-9870-7 (pbk.) — ISBN 978-1-4358-9871-4 (6-pack)
1. Obama, Barack—Family—Juvenile literature. 2. Presidents—United States—Family—Juvenile literature. 3. Obama, Michelle, 1964—Juvenile literature. 4. Obama, Malia, 1998—Juvenile literature. 5. Obama, Sasha, 2001—Juvenile literature. I. Title.
  E909.Z87 2010
  973.932092—dc22
                                        2009036516

Manufactured in the United States of America

CPSIA Compltance Information: Batch #WW10PK: For Further Information contact Rosen Publishing, New York, New York at 1-800-237-9932

Contents

Meet the First Family

Do you know who the president of the United States is? If you answered Barack Obama, you are right! President Obama lives with his family in the White House. This big house in Washington, D.C., has been the home of American presidents and their families since 1800. Today, President Obama lives there with his wife, Michelle, and his daughters, Malia and Sasha. Michelle's mother, Marian Robinson, moved into the White House, too, so she could help take care of the girls.

The president's family is called the first family. There have been many first families. The Obamas, however, are the first African-American first family.

Here the first family is shown waving to visitors and reporters from a White House balcony in April 2009.

Inspiring Others

Before Barack Obama became president, the Obamas lived in Chicago, Illinois. There, Obama was **elected** to the Illinois state senate in 1996 and to the U.S. Senate, in 2004.

In July 2004, Obama spoke at the **Democratic** National **Convention**, where people pick the Democratic Party's **candidate** for president. Obama spoke about how his father came from Kenya and his mother from Kansas. Obama said that he was thankful to be American and that "in no other country on Earth is my story even possible." His speech **inspired** many people. Obama decided to run for president himself. He began his **campaign** in May 2007.

Obama was still an Illinois state senator when he spoke at the Democratic National Convention in 2004.

Becoming the Forty-fourth President

Obama traveled across the country, explaining his dream for America. Obama argued that it was time to change how the government worked, and he offered "change we can believe in." Voters decided that they believed in him. Obama won the presidential election on November 4, 2008.

The following January brought changes for the Obama family. They moved to Washington, D.C., which meant Malia and Sasha would go to a new school. Their father gave up his seat in the Senate. On January 20, 2009, Barack Obama became the forty-fourth president of the United States. Countless people watched this event in person and on TV.

Here Barack Obama gives his first speech after becoming president. The president's first speech is called an inaugural address.

Living in the White House

Once Obama became president, he and his family moved into the White House. The White House is huge. It has 132 rooms. It even has a movie theater! The rooms where the president's family lives are in the middle part of the building.

The house's East Wing has offices for Michelle, who is the First Lady, and the people who work for her. Barack Obama and his closest **advisers** have offices in the West Wing. The president's office is called the Oval Office because it is oval shaped. Presidents often give speeches, many of which are shown on TV, in the Oval Office.

It takes 570 gallons (2,158 L) of paint to give the outside of the White House a new coat of paint. Shown here is the White House's north lawn.

Keeping the Obamas Safe

Though the White House is the Obamas' home, it is also one of the world's best-known buildings. Thousands of people visit the White House each year. Some people even tour parts of the house. However, the first family must be kept safe there. Today, many people **protect** President Obama and his family.

The group in charge of protecting the president and his family is called the Secret Service. Members of the Secret Service walk the grounds of the White House looking for people who should not be there. Secret Service members also travel almost everywhere with the Obamas.

Sasha and Malia travel in Secret Service sport-utility vehicles, or SUVs, to school. Here, a member of the Secret Service opens a door for Sasha.

The President's Day

The U.S. president is one of the world's busiest people. President Obama generally wakes up at around six thirty in the morning. He exercises and spends time with his daughters before getting to work. Each morning, Obama reads reports from his advisers about problems in the United States and around the world. After that, Obama meets with his advisers and with other government leaders.

Sometimes, Obama sets time aside to talk to reporters or to meet with visiting leaders from other countries. Other days he will look over or sign a bill that **Congress** has passed. Once a president signs a bill, it becomes a law.

This picture shows President Obama signing an order about scientific studies in the East Room of the White House in March 2009.

The First Lady's Day

Like her husband, Michelle Obama is very busy. As the First Lady, she is the hostess of the White House. This means that she has to greet and look after any important people who visit the White House. As First Lady, Michelle pushes for issues that are important to her, too. She wants to help working mothers and military families. Michelle also hopes to inspire more people around the country to **volunteer** in their communities.

Michelle sets aside time to spend with Malia and Sasha, too. She has said that raising her daughters is her most important job.

Here the First Lady and the president are shown greeting people at a volunteer event in Washington, D.C.

Kids in the White House

Though their father is the president, Malia and Sasha Obama's lives are like those of other kids in many ways. They have to do chores and go to school. As several other presidents' kids have, Malia and Sasha go to the Sidwell Friends School. Since their mother and father are busy, their grandmother often cares for them.

There are **advantages** to being the president's children, too. In summer 2009, Barack and Michelle took Malia and Sasha to Europe and Africa. The girls saw interesting sights and met powerful world leaders. Malia and Sasha also get to meet big stars, such as the Jonas Brothers.

Here Sasha and Malia play an Easter game on the White House's south lawn. The Easter Egg Roll takes place at the White House every year.

First Family Fun

The Obamas are a close family, and they try to spend as much time together as they can. One place they spend time together is Camp David, in Maryland. Camp David is the U.S. president's country home. It has a swimming pool, woods to walk in, and plenty of peace and quiet.

The Obamas have fun at the White House, too. On the night he was elected, Barack Obama promised his daughters that he would get them a dog. In April 2009, Senator Ted Kennedy and his wife gave the family a Portuguese water dog. The Obamas named the dog Bo.

This picture shows the Obamas taking their dog, Bo, out for a walk on the White House lawn. Bo is sometimes called the first dog.

Feeling at Home in Washington, D.C.

Though the move to Washington, D.C., was a big change for them, the Obamas quickly settled into the White House. In the Oval Office, Barack signed bills to help the **economy** and to make sure that women are paid fairly. Michelle helped plant a vegetable garden at the White House. She and Barack visited Europe, got along well with world leaders, and won praise from reporters. Malia and Sasha made friends at their new school. Their grandmother enjoyed going to concerts and school events.

No one knows what the **future** holds for the Obamas. However, they have already changed how people picture America's first family.

advantages (ud-VAN-tij-ez) Benefits from something.

advisers (ed-VY-zurz) People who help you make decisions.

campaign (kam-PAYN) A plan to get a certain result, such as to win an election.

candidate (KAN-dih-dayt) A person who runs in an election.

Congress (KON-gres) The part of the U.S. government that makes laws.

convention (kun-VEN-shun) A meeting for some special purpose.

Democratic (deh-muh-KRA-tik) Having to do with one of the two major political parties in the United States.

economy (ih-KAH-nuh-mee) The way in which a country or a business oversees its goods and services.

elected (ee-LEK-tid) Picked for an office by voters.

future (FYOO-chur) The time that is coming.

inspired (in-SPY-urd) Moved.

protect (pruh-TEKT) To keep safe.

volunteer (vah-lun-TEER) To give one's time without pay.

Index

Web Sites

Due to the changing nature of Internet links, PowerKids Press has developed an online list of Web sites related to the subject of this book. This site is updated regularly. Please use this link to access the list:
www.powerkidslinks.com/obamas/family/